The Nature Kid's Guide to
BACKYARD BIRDS

DAVID ANDERSON

LP Media Inc. Publishing
Text copyright © 2026 by LP Media Inc.
All rights reserved.

For information address LP Media Inc. Publishing,
30012 Variolite St NW, Princeton MN 55371
www.lpmedia.org

Publication Data

Backyard Birds
The Nature Kid's Guide to Backyard Birds — First edition.

Summary: "Learn all about Bird watching, the Nature Kid Way"
— Provided by publisher.

ISBN: 979-8-89818-209-0

[1. Backyard Birds – Non-Fiction] I. Title.

Title: The Nature Kid's Guide to Backyard Birds

CONTENTS

Backyard Wonders 4

Feather Features 6

Tweet Tweet 8

Backyard Bounty 10

Red Birds 12

Hovering Jewels 14

Brilliant Blues 16

The Early Bird 18

Oriole Orange 20

Rainbow Rascal 22

Goldfinch Glow 24

Pileated Power 26

Bluebird Comeback 28

Waxwing Wonders 30

Clever Crows 32

Silent Striker 34

Helping Habitats 36

Backyard Brilliance 38

BACKYARD WONDERS

Over 900 types of birds live in North America. How many can you count in your yard?

Chirp! A happy robin lands on a backyard fence.

There are amazing birds living right outside your window. They nest in your trees, splash in your puddles, and sing from your fence posts every single morning. You may have seen them a hundred times without really even noticing them.

Robins are a great example. They love yards with short grass and spend their mornings hunting for worms, tilting their heads to listen for movement just below the surface. Spot one and you are already a bird watcher!

Birds need food, water, and safe spots to rest. Your yard can give them all three. The more you look, the more you will find.

FEATHER FEATURES

Bird feathers are made of keratin — the same stuff as your fingernails!

Fluff! A cardinal puffs up its bright feathers to stay warm.

Feathers might seem ordinary, but they do some amazing things for birds. Feathers help birds fly, stay dry, and keep warm in cold weather.

Birds have several different kinds of feathers. Soft, fluffy **down feathers** sit close to the skin for warmth. Long wing feathers help with flying. Tail feathers work like a rudder to help birds steer through the air.

Feathers wear out over time, so birds grow new ones each year. This is called molting. Old feathers fall out, and fresh ones grow in to take their place. It's like getting new clothes every year!

TWEET TWEET

FUN FACT!

A mockingbird can learn and copy over 200 different songs in its lifetime!

Tweet! A yellow warbler fills the morning with its song.

Birds sing for many reasons. Some sing to find a **mate**. Others sing to say, 'This spot is mine!' Each kind of bird has its own special song.

Birds also use calls to talk to each other. A short, sharp call can mean danger is near. A soft peep might say, 'I am right here.' Baby birds call out loudly when they want food.

Some birds learn their songs from their parents. Young birds listen carefully and practice again and again. That is how they learn to sing, just like you learn new things by practicing!

BACKYARD BOUNTY

Crunch! A blue jay cracks open a seed at the feeder.

Birds really only need three things: food, water, and safe places to nest. Gardens and yards can give them all of these.

Many birds eat seeds, bugs, and berries. They find food in grass, on trees, and at feeders. A birdbath gives them a place to drink and splash around to clean themselves. Birds love fresh water!

When it is time to raise a family, birds build nests in trees, bushes, and even on porches. They use twigs, grass, and mud. A good nest keeps eggs warm and babies safe from danger.

RED BIRDS

The cardinal is the state bird of seven U.S. states — more than any other bird!

Chip! A bright red cardinal calls from a snowy branch.

Northern Cardinals are easy to spot. The male is bright red from head to tail. The female is a soft brown with a red beak and a tall, pointed **crest**.

Cardinals do not fly south in winter. They stay in the same area all year long. On a snowy day, a red cardinal against white snow really stands out!

These birds love sunflower seeds. They crack them open with their strong, cone-shaped beaks. Cardinals often visit feeders at sunrise and sunset, so those are the best times to watch for them.

HOVERING JEWELS

A hummingbird's heart can beat over 1,200 times in just one minute!

Buzz! A tiny hummingbird zooms right up to a bright red flower.

Ruby-throated Hummingbirds are one of the smallest birds you will see. They weigh less than a nickel — only about 3 grams! The male has a shiny red throat that glows like a jewel in the sun.

These birds can **hover** in the air like tiny helicopters. Their wings beat about 53 times per second. They can even fly backward, something most birds cannot do.

Hummingbirds drink nectar from flowers. Their long, thin beaks fit right inside the blooms. A single hummingbird visits hundreds of flowers every day to get enough energy.

BRILLIANT BLUES

16

Jay! Jay! A bold blue jay screams from the oak tree.

Blue jays are loud, bold, and surprisingly smart. They have bright blue feathers marked with white and black, and a tall crest on top of their head that rises and falls with their mood.

These clever birds can copy the calls of hawks perfectly. Other birds hear the fake alarm and scatter, clearing the way for the jay to swoop in and grab the best food!

Blue jays hide thousands of acorns in the ground each fall. They often forget where they buried them, and those forgotten acorns grow into new oak trees. Blue jays accidentally plant forests without even trying!

THE EARLY BIRD

Tug! An American robin pulls a wiggly worm from the soil.

American Robins are one of the most common birds you will see in your backyard. They have a rusty orange chest and a dark gray back. You can spot them hopping across lawns, stopping to look and listen.

Robins tilt their heads to hear worms moving underground. When they hear one, they grab it fast! They also eat berries and small bugs.

In spring, the female robin builds a cozy nest using mud and dry grass. Inside, she lays 3-5 beautiful blue eggs. Robin eggs are so famous for their color that people named a shade of blue after them!

ORIOLE ORANGE

Whistle! A flash of orange sails across the summer sky.

Baltimore Orioles are bright orange and black. The male looks like a flying flame! These colorful birds spend summer in the eastern US states.

Orioles build amazing hanging nests that look like pouches. The female weaves them from plant fibers and string, working for up to a week. The finished nests swing from the tips of tree branches.

In fall, orioles fly south to Central America. They travel thousands of miles to stay warm. When spring returns, they come right back to the same trees where they nested before!

RAINBOW RASCAL

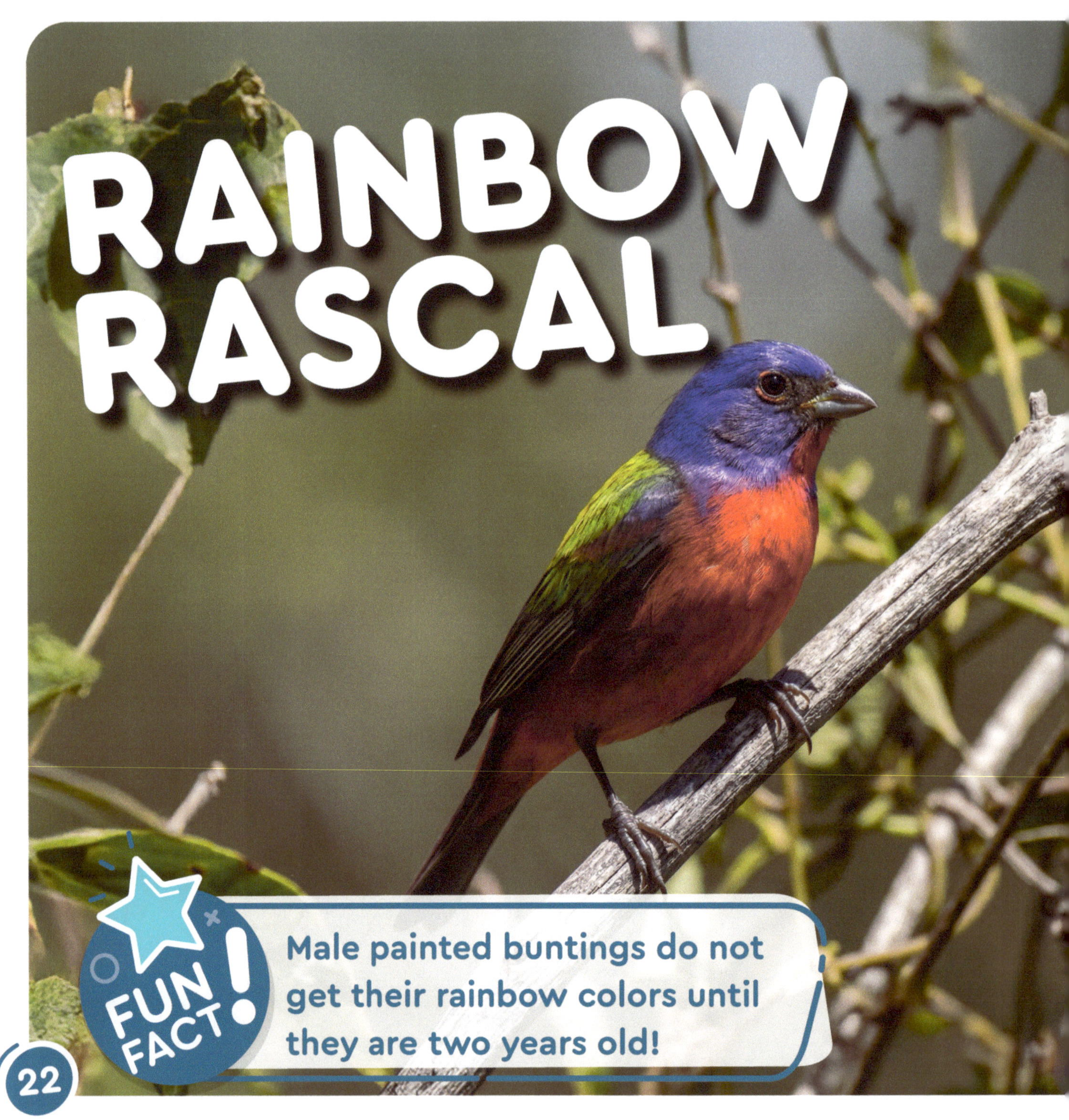

Flash! A painted bunting glows like a living rainbow.

Painted Buntings are tiny birds with big color. The male has a blue head, a green back, and a bright red chest. No other North American bird has so many bold colors!

Females are a soft green color. This helps them hide in bushes near their nests, since green feathers look just like leaves. Staying hidden keeps them safe.

These small birds live in the southern United States. They like thick bushes and tangled vines where they can stay out of sight. Buntings eat seeds and small bugs they find near the ground.

GOLDFINCH GLOW
DID YOU KNOW?
Goldfinches wait until July to nest — later than almost any other North American bird!
24

Swoop! A golden bird dips and lands on a branch.

American Goldfinches are bright yellow with black wings. They fly up and down in a bouncy, roller-coaster way. People sometimes call them 'wild canaries' because of their cheerful color.

In winter, their feathers change. Males turn from bright yellow to dull olive brown. When spring comes, they molt and glow gold again like magic.

Goldfinches love thistle seeds. They eat mostly seeds all year long, which is unusual. Few other birds do that! They even feed seeds to their babies instead of bugs.

PILEATED POWER

A pileated woodpecker's tongue is so long it wraps around the back of its skull!

Wham! A large woodpecker hammers a hole in a dead tree.

Pileated Woodpeckers are big, bold birds. They are about the size of a crow — nearly 19 inches long! A bright red crest sits on top of their head like a pointed cap.

These powerful birds peck into dead wood to find bugs. They love carpenter ants most of all. Their strong beaks chip away bark and dig deep, rectangular holes.

The holes they make help other animals, too. Owls, ducks, and bats move into old woodpecker holes. One bird's hard work becomes another animal's cozy home!

BLUEBIRD COMEBACK

Flick! A hungry bluebird scans the yard for bugs to catch.

Eastern Bluebirds have sky-blue feathers and a warm orange chest. They sit on fence posts and low branches, watching the ground below. From there, they spot bugs to catch.

Years ago, bluebird numbers dropped badly. Other birds took over their nesting spots, and there were fewer places to raise families. People began putting up special nest boxes to help.

The nest boxes worked! Bluebirds found safe places to raise their young again. Today, their numbers are growing. It is one of nature's great success stories.

WAXWING WONDERS

Zing! A sleek waxwing plucks a berry from a branch.

Cedar Waxwings are smooth, silky birds. They have fine brown feathers, a black mask, and a yellow-tipped tail. Tiny red waxy dots on their wing tips give them their name. They are so beautiful they almost don't look real!

These birds love berries more than almost anything. A whole **flock** can strip a bush clean in just minutes! They follow the ripest fruit from tree to tree all year long.

Waxwings share food with each other in a special way. They sometimes pass berries back and forth along a branch. It is one of the sweetest sights in nature.

CLEVER CROWS
DID YOU KNOW?
Crows can give gifts! They sometimes bring shiny objects to people who feed them.

Caw! Caw! A shiny black crow swoops down to the sidewalk.

American Crows are some of the smartest birds alive. They are all black from beak to tail, with glossy feathers that shine in the sun. You can find them almost anywhere in North America.

Crows can solve tricky problems and use tools. They drop nuts on roads so cars crack them open! Scientists have found that crows remember human faces for years.

Crows live in family groups. Young crows stay home and help their parents raise new babies. At night, big flocks gather in trees to sleep together for safety.

SILENT STRIKER

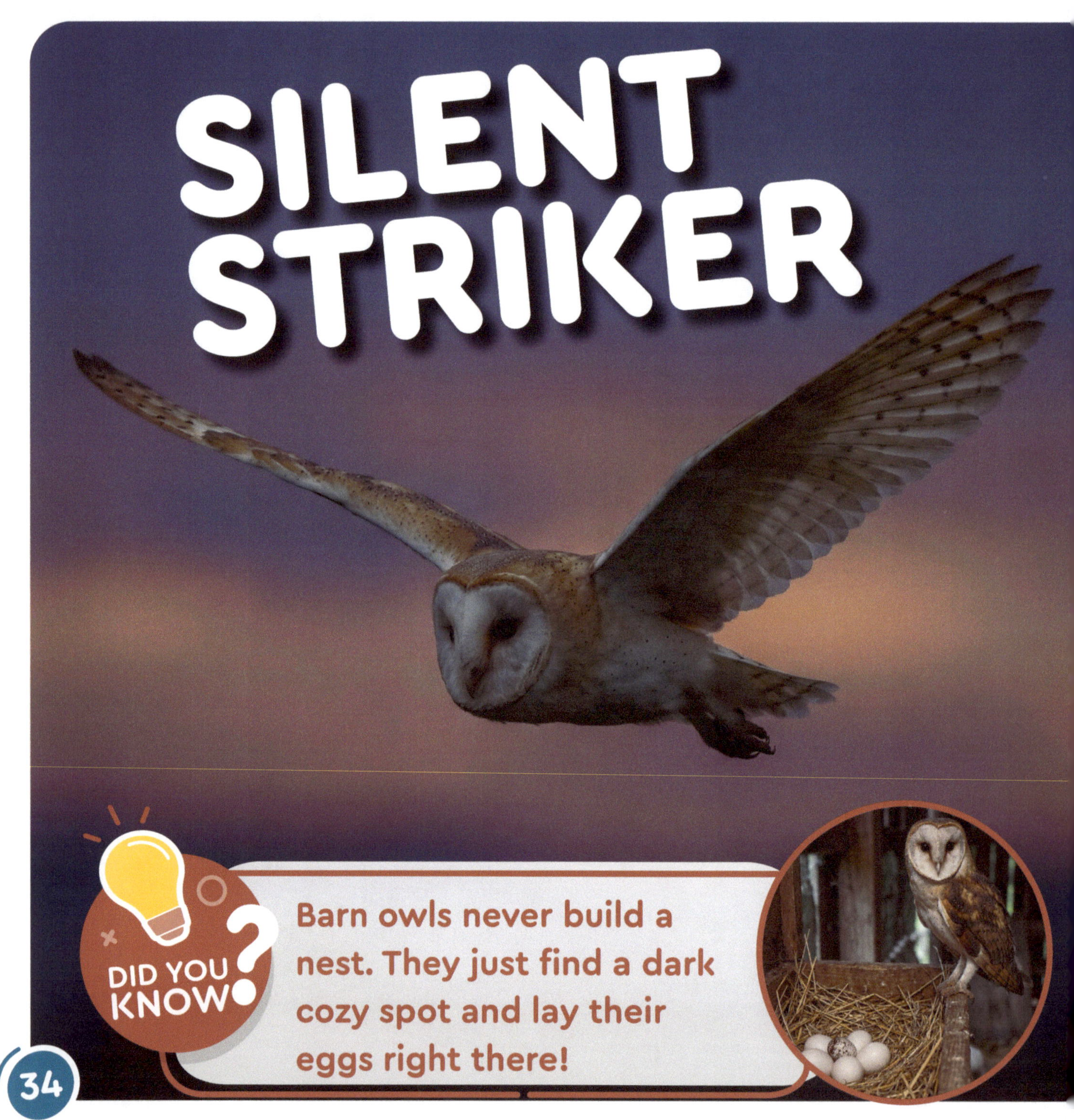

Barn owls never build a nest. They just find a dark cozy spot and lay their eggs right there!

Whoosh! A pale barn owl glides through the sky at dusk.

Barn Owls are night hunters with heart-shaped faces. Their white and tan feathers glow in the moonlight. Large dark eyes help them see in very low light.

These owls fly without making a sound. Soft edges on their feathers break up the noise of flight. A mouse on the ground never hears them coming until it is too late.

Barn Owls often nest in old barns and church towers, but they also use tree holes. One owl family can catch thousands of mice each year, making them great helpers for farmers!

HELPING HABITATS

Black oil sunflower seeds attract more backyard bird species than any other food!

Click! A bluebird climbs into a birdhouse on a tall fence post.

There are several easy ways you can help birds right in your neighborhood. Hang a feeder filled with bird seed near a window. Keep it clean and full, and birds will find it fast!

Planting flowers and bushes gives birds food and shelter. Native plants work best because local birds already know how to use them. Even a small garden patch makes a real difference.

Keep cats indoors to keep birds safe. Pick up trash that could hurt them. Every small act adds up, and the birds in your yard will be better off because of it!

BACKYARD BRILLIANCE

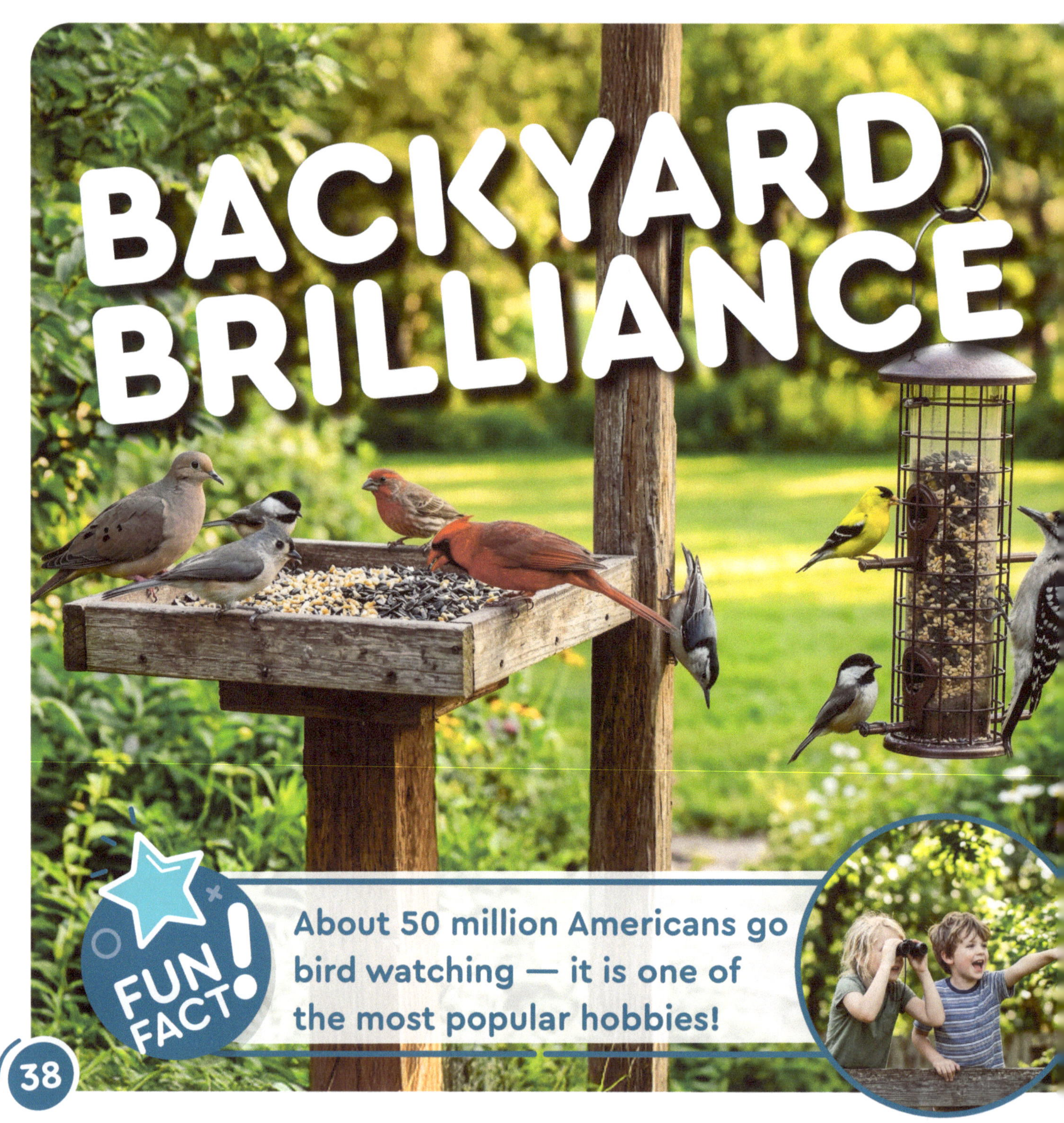

Peep! A world of wonder waits just outside your door.

You are ready to become a real bird watcher! All you need is a quiet spot, a little patience, and your own two eyes. Early morning is the best time to start, when birds are most active and singing their loudest.

Pick one bird and really watch it. How does it move? What does it eat? Does it share, or does it chase others away? The more you observe, the more you will learn!

Keep a notebook and write down what you see. Draw the birds you spot. Over time, you will get to know them like old friends who visit every single day!

GLOSSARY

crest

A tuft of feathers that stands up on top of a bird's head

down feathers

Soft, fluffy feathers close to a bird's skin that keep it warm

flock

A group of birds that travel or eat together

hover

To stay in one spot in the air by beating wings fast

mate

A partner that helps make a family and raise babies

www.ingramcontent.com/pod-product-compliance
Lightning Source LLC
Chambersburg PA
CBHW041609110726
48005CB00002B/341